The Grass is Greener on the Other Side, But it's Synthetic!

Jeremy Michael Allen, Sr.

Copyright © 2019 by Jeremy Michael Allen, Sr.

The Grass is Greener on the Other Side, But it's Synthetic!
by Jeremy Michael Allen, Sr.

Printed in the United States of America

All rights reserved solely by the author. The author guarantees all contents are original and do not infringe upon the legal rights of any other person or work. No part of this book may be reproduced in any form without the permission of the author. The views expressed in this book are not necessarily those of the publisher.

www.JacksonPublish.com

This book is dedicated to my father, Reverend Joseph Allen of Eutaw, Alabama. My dad died on June 12, 2017, after a year-long, hard-fought battle with cancer and being paralyzed. Even in my dad's last days, he continued fighting and ensuring and prioritizing everyone else's happiness. The month before he died, with what little voice he had left, he asked a nurse, "are you doing ok today?" She replied, "Rev. Allen, I am ok, but I could be better," he then said, "I want to pray with you." He never wanted it to be about *him*; he was a true illustration of humble love. As an only child, I take great responsibility and pride in representing my father and continuing to rely on all the multitude of lessons he taught me. I am immensely proud to have had you in my life to guide me, discipline me (sometimes in ways I don't care to remember), and give me examples of love. Dad, I love you and miss you deeply every day. I thank my mother Roxanne Allen for selecting such an amazing man.

This book serves as a part of the legacy you left in me. Lives will be changed, and people will receive help in their businesses, marriages, and most of all their daily walks.

TABLE OF CONTENTS

The Start: New Home, New Grass, New Problems....1

Chapter One: Know the Seed...................11

Chapter Two: The Roots Matter More
than the Results.............................23

Chapter Three: Stop Cutting So Short,
and Know Your Environment...................39

Chapter Four: Rest, Heal, and Re-seed...........47

Chapter Five: Synthetic is Not Real -
You Know that, Right?.......................53

The Start

NEW HOME, NEW GRASS, NEW PROBLEMS

In 2001, I was blessed to purchase my first home, along with my beautiful wife. As you can imagine, as a first-time, eager homeowner, I quickly created a plan of attack for the grass/yard. I wanted my yard to be immaculate, one that produced "WOWs!" from onlookers in the neighborhood. So, I went and bought the best lawn mower and weed eater, all kinds of fertilizer: Weed and Feed, Grub GONE, Miracle Grow, and anything else that *looked* cool. I had the best hose and sprinkler system that money could buy and, of course, I had mulch, stone, and pavers to edge the lawn from the flower bed to the

The Grass is Greener on the Other Side, But it's Synthetic!

front door. I was ready!! I carefully read instructions, and I researched online to see what others were doing in my area to have great yards. I set off to begin the task at-hand and had a 30-day goal of fixing up this poor looking yard. As time progressed, I noticed some improvements: the grass began to grow, it was greener, and certainly looked thicker and healthier. Just as I prepared for the first cut, it rained, and I was unable to cut the yard. I decided to wait 24 hours for the yard to dry, and then use my new self-propelled Toro Express mower. I was so proud of this lawn mower! There I was, all set to go; my fist real cut after getting the grass greener, thicker, and much healthier than before. I spent roughly 3 hours cutting a yard that most people cut in 20 minutes. Remember, I wanted an immaculate yard! I put lines in it, and made a little design in the center. I used the new weed eater so well that people walked by smiling, and gave me the thumbs up sign. I knew I was on to something! I discarded all the lawn clippings and used a blower for all the small things

I missed. As the sun set, the yard looked amazing, and I set out to address the kitchen next, which also needed some extra TLC.

Yup, I called it! The neighbors came by to visit and welcome us to the area; they began commenting on the yard as soon as they approached. It was a major success, and I was so happy, but something really strange began to happen. About three days after my first cut, the grass started showing brown/burnt-looking patches in the yard. It looked like a dairy cow on the hillside, and I was very upset! I kept watering the lawn; I even used more Miracle Grow, but it didn't seem to work. I took a break from the products for a while and decided I needed to give the yard time to heal. I cut the grass two or three more times, but it wasn't improving, it was getting worse. I had all the best tools money could buy; I bought the best yard chemicals, but it was to no avail. After 45 days, the entire yard was dead; all the grass died!

I remember sitting at the kitchen table with my wife, a native of Brooklyn, New York, who could've cared less if we had grass or not. Frustrated, I told her, "it can't be this hard!" Skip, Fitz, Ed, and Mr. Phelps all had awesome looking yards, and I never saw them doing much of anything special like I had. I was out there practically killing myself 10–15 hours a week on this yard, and it was almost dead. Like every great wife, I remember her saying, "so just leave it alone, no one really cares anyway, it'll be snowing soon." Are you serious, leave it alone? No, not me! I wasn't raised that way. I was not going to let this simple yard beat me and kept reminding myself, I am way too good to be defeated by this. I spent the next several months fixing the yard, investing hundreds of dollars and hundreds of hours in time and effort. Finally, it was mid-August, and I'd gotten the yard back to where I needed it to be. There was only one problem; one small issue arose. My employer, the United States Navy, wanted me to leave in one week to deploy on a

U.S. Submarine for a 95-day mission (during these missions, you have zero contact with anyone). Not only was I sad to leave my family, I was mad about my grass. I know, I know, it's just grass. I wish it were that easy. So, my family and I decided that we would ask some folks from the church to come by and cut the grass during the time I'd be away (**never ask church friends to cut grass, never.** *Inside joke*). As the 95 days underwater passed, all I could think about was my family, my new home and, of course, I wondered if the church folks were loving my grass like I did. Before I left, I gave great instructions, I went over everything, and I even told them how I had just revived the yard.

I remember my wife picking me up at the airport, and after all the mushy stuff and small talk of catching up, I asked, "so, how's the yard?" Not only did she almost flip out, she nearly hit me. "You mean to tell me within the first hour of you being back on U.S. soil, that's all you can think about." I interrupted her and said "Yes, soil. My grass; did they do a good job?" That was not a pleasant ride home, nor did she ever answer the question. No worries though, we only lived a short distance from the airport, and I was about to see how the yard looked for myself. Although it was nearing 10pm, I remember getting home, grabbing a flashlight and going outside to see my beautiful….. "You have got to $&*%$# kidding me!" Oh my god, there is no way anyone can cut grass like this, I mean, I had a grass catcher on the mower, and clearly they didn't use that. I also left a weed eater and had the edges trimmed up nicely before I left. All they had to do was follow the lead I left. Lines, yeah there were lines, but they were all over the yard as if a blind man had cut it. I was pissed! I was so hurt and angry that someone really thought this was acceptable in any fashion. Clearly, they don't care about their yard or anything else in life, I thought. I remember walking into the house and, to my wife, I asked, "what did they do?" She told me they came by every two weeks and even brought their own mower. His own mower, NO! You can't cut it every two weeks; it was supposed to be cut every week and with *my* mower! I had my blades set and sharpened especially for *my* yard. His mower was probably set for his yard or, by looking at the grass, his mower wasn't set at all. I explained to her that he didn't use the grass catcher, his blades were dull, and he probably cut way too low because I could see the dirt. Wooooo, I was hot! I couldn't wait to wake up the next morning to go outside and look more closely at the major mistake this man made in my yard.

After waking, I walked outside and unfortunately, just as I figured, everything was what I expected. He cut my yard way too low, waited too long in between cuts, and his blades were dull as butter knives. I know my neighbors were laughing. I know they knew how upset I had to be. One guy stopped by and said, "I started to tell your guy to stop cutting because I would do it, but I didn't feel comfortable saying that." You see, everyone knew how impressive I wanted my yard to be. They knew I wanted great curb appeal. I wanted my yard to say *hello* when you drove by, but this yard was saying, *man my stomach hurts, and I feel like I'm about to throw up.*

As time went on that next year, I had to rent a backhoe and dig up all the grass, bring in new dirt, and put down sod. I spent about $3,000, but I was determined to get this yard right. I worked for three days straight installing all the sod myself and had to ask the truck driver who delivered it how to install it. I was clueless. I was determined to do it though, and that is exactly what I did. Within 72 hours, I had a new yard with beautiful edges and green grass. Months went by, and everyone was back to admiring my grass, but there was one problem. I had a pool of water that settled in the front yard that had never been there before; thus, giving the grass too much water and eventually killing it. Now, I had no one to blame but me. Who knew I was supposed to slope the yard for drainage? Not me. It was at this point in my life where I almost gave in.

You see, the water was such an issue that the steps to my home began to cave in and detach from the house. As a homeowner, the last thing you want to happen to your home is foundation issues. My wife had no idea I was losing it deep inside, but I couldn't show her. I had to remain strong and act like I knew what I was doing, but I honestly had no clue at all. At this point, I was willing to do what 90% of men would never do; I called a landscaper and asked him to come help me. I remember when John showed up from AMG and told me exactly what my issue was and how I could fix it ASAP. I pleaded to him, "please don't charge me an arm and a leg, as I just spent well over $5,000 to get this yard right." After a payment of about $2,500, John had the water issue fixed and had my yard looking back to new. What a costly mistake on my part for installing my own dirt and sod without putting in the proper slope/grading under it. Not only did I pay John, I also had to pay to replace my steps and several yards of concrete, which cost me over $3,000. After five years of being in this home, I had spent well over $10,000 trying to get my grass greener.

Chapter One
KNOW THE SEED

Anything that has a life cycle must also have a seed, or a form of a seed. This is especially true when it comes to growing your yard/grass. When I first started attacking my new yard at my new home, the biggest challenge for me was, I had no idea what seeds were already planted. The results I inherited were solely based on the seeds planted by the previous owners. Although I could water the yard, and fertilize it, I still had no control over the seed that was planted, until I removed the old seed and planted my own.

In life, the same is very true. When you enter a career, marriage, or any situation that is already established, you have not planted the seed; therefore, you must live with the results. It's very important that you understand the power of planting seeds and seeds that can take root. Like a great-looking yard, a great life, career, and marriage all start with planting seeds. There is a saying we hear all the time, but often we fall far from it: you reap what you sow. This passage not only has meaning in planting seeds for fruit trees, vegetables, and other crops, but also life. In any successful thing you take part in, you must sow a seed of positivity, determination, dedication, endurance, patience, and several other things. It's so important to understand the seeds that you sow and to sow them in strategic ways.

I personally don't sow the same seeds in every situation that I encounter. I also try to understand the seeds that have already been put in place prior to me walking into something. The biggest issue I had with my first yard was, I never took the time to evaluate the soil, the seeds, and the condition of the yard under the surface. I jumped right in based on what I saw on the surface, and I assumed the fertilizer and chemicals that I was using to treat the yard would have worked. Wrong! Let me encourage you in this; don't look at careers, marriages, and life on the surface and think you can figure things out. The biggest issue I run into with business owners that I mentor is, they see what Dwayne, Tom, Shelia, or Carlos are doing, and they think, *oh, I can do that; I can jump in and run a company and do just what they are doing, or do it better.* Not once do they look at the seeds CEOs have sown, or the work they put into the soil they are rooted in. This was especially true in my government contracting days.

I recall a meeting with a small startup company that had a CEO who was very strong in IT/software development. This CEO just left a larger company to start his own business because he saw how much money others were making and thought, *I can do that* (how many times do we hear that). I would later witness that same

CEO almost lose his house and marriage because he had no idea how to run a company. Sure, he knew software development better than anyone else I had ever met and, frankly, everyone at our agency knew he was the best. But he couldn't tell you the difference between a W-2, a 1099, or a special at Chick-fil-A for $5.99 (Chick-fil-A never has specials). Realistically, that is normal and very understandable; most CEOs can't elaborate on the nuanced details of every part of a company, but they certainly better have some knowledge and familiarity.

It wasn't until this CEO began bringing in others who were subject matter experts (SMEs) that he realized how much he was really missing. These experts came in and planted seeds. They had a mission and focused only on the things that mattered to them. Whether it was Human Resources, Finance, Business Development, or any other specific business focus, these SMEs knew what seeds to plant and where to plant them. The CEO then realized his role had shifted; he was now planting the right people in the right place to grow the company.

It's very critical that you know what your best seeds are and to sow them accordingly. Being good at something does not mean you can be the leader of that area. Most of us get extremely happy when we obtain a glimpse of success and then want to immediately own something or start our own venture. We never really knew the details or the true functions, but we tasted a little success, and now we have become experts. WRONG! In that same vein, some people have natural God-given gifts and talents. No matter what the task is, they can jump in and execute things with no practice, no preparation, and sometimes no energy; and they are just blessed! But even those people can't be great unless they utilize the seed correctly. I have seen some very talented singers, dancers, and musicians take their God-given gift and turn it in a wrong direction so fast. They started sowing seeds in soil that would eventually kill them. So, your question at this point is, how do I know what my seed is? Very good question, I am so glad you asked. Let me explain.

Your seed is that feeling you get when you do something, and your heart/passion is in it so much you could care less about anything else. Athletes normally pick this up at a very young age; mainly because they are coached this way, but also because they love sports so much, that it's all they think about. A great example of this is the golf icon, Tiger Woods. Whether you like him or not, his work ethic became his seed. Tiger would hit 2,000–3,000 golf balls a day to perfect his swing. He understood he was good at golf, but he wanted to be the greatest. He studied, he practiced, he adopted a very strict diet, and he even had a set bed time to ensure his body was properly rested and ready for all conditions.

Tiger mastered the art of true dedication to his craft. As a result, he achieved success on the golf course, and that success led him to millions of dollars off the golf course (endorsements, events, and other opportunities that paid him millions). I believe you must sow your seeds very wisely, but you certainly must know what your seeds are. Here is another example; I will use me this time, as this is my book (lol). When I was a kid, I loved to talk. I loved to make people laugh; I loved to see people happy. My joy came from others' joy and making their lives better. I also loved to work. Seriously, I loved working 12-15 hours a day, doing all kinds of jobs. Since the age of 13, I loved cutting grass (I bet you knew that already). I loved washing cars, trimming trees, building things, and helping my dad with any and all construction projects.

At that time, I had no idea what my seed was. I just knew I loved helping others, and I loved making money. It wasn't until my second year in the Navy that I realized I had the skills, expertise, and desires of an entrepreneur, but not just an average entrepreneur. I wanted to help others and let them gain success through my success. I also noticed that my seed was networking and utilizing my gift of conversation. Who knew in 1995 when I was suspended from school for three days for yelling out in class, talking too much, and talking back, that one day I could use talking to help me make millions?

I will never forget Mr. Joe Powell looking me in my face and telling me, "Jeremy Allen, you will never be anything in life; you talk too much and you are not smart at all." I don't fault him for making that statement; actually I am thrilled he made that statement. It's statements like that, that I use every time I sit at a table and sign a deal, build a business, or when I put my daughter through college. That voice often comes in my head and nudges me to dig a little deeper. I found that my seed was there all along, but I had to recognize it and really manifest it. I also needed to plant it in the correct places to see the growth I was expecting.

The seed you are seeking is there, it's already inside you. Many of us have multiple seeds, and we gain access to more and more seeds as we sow more and more. The key to finding your true seed, or your true passion, is taking the first steps toward beginning something new. Try things, conduct research, join clubs, groups, or volunteer organizations; don't just sit back and say, *I don't have a seed to sow.*

Although I am not in the construction field, I thoroughly enjoy building and helping others. In 2000, I had the honor of leading a group of Midshipmen from the U.S. Naval Academy and other Navy-enlisted personnel in building the first all-volunteer, all Navy-built home for a low-income family in Annapolis, Maryland through Habitat for Humanity. When I planted that seed every Saturday for five months, I never would have thought that through that seed, I would meet the Governor of Maryland, which resulted in me being well connected in the local business community. During that time, I had no desire to own my own company, I had only been in the Navy for three years, and I was just starting to really enjoy it.

Later that year, I had the opportunity to purchase a family-owned sports store. Wow! Talk about rapid growth. When I planted that seed in Annapolis, I didn't anticipate the growth of a business. Not only did that seed blossom from there, it led to 10 great years of business, multiple locations, and the store eventually employed over 60 staff members. We were recognized at a sports conference in Las Vegas as the *Best Sports Store* in Maryland. I personally attribute a lot of that success to planting seeds for a family who needed a home, and as a result, I reaped fruit in the form of monetary funds to purchase a new home.

So, let me end this chapter with this: planting seeds is very important to success and growth, but what's more important is to know what you're planting and to plant it in the proper places. Here are some steps to consider:

1. Take some time and look at the seed you have. Are you happy with it?

2. Listen for opportunities to plant your seed (it may be uncomfortable sometimes).

3. Once you plant your seed, give it time to grow; don't pull it up and move on, let it take root.

4. Everyone doesn't need to know about your seed. Stop thinking you must tell everyone. Plant your seed and give it the proper care; it will grow, and they will see it.

Chapter Two

THE ROOTS MATTER MORE THAN THE RESULTS

Oftentimes when I speak with young business owners, or newly married couples, the first thing I hear from them is, *I want what you have.* Huh? *I want to experience life as you and your family have; I want my results to look like yours.* I am always humbled that the display of fruit is showing in such a positive way that others seek and desire my results, but then my mind immediately questions the root of this. I then begin to think, *do they really want this?* I've even asked my two oldest children who are now 21 and 18, *do you really want this, do you want the fruit or the process to get the fruit?*

You see, my roots started when I was about 12 years old. My parents and I were living in Huguenot, New York where my parents had awesome jobs with remarkable incomes. My parents were attending a church service on a Sunday evening and a guest minister, Pastor Bill Parks, was ministering about his mission trips to Mexico. Following that service, my father felt the urge to follow Rev./Pastor Parks and his team to Mexico to experience and try out one of the trips for himself. Not only did he try it, my parents quickly sold their home, packed up everything we owned, and we moved to Eutaw, Alabama all within eight months. They were going to be missionaries to Mexico via Eutaw, Alabama. Now, this was not only a huge adjustment for me, this was also a huge adjustment for my mother as well. You see—then in 1990 and now in 2019—Eutaw, Alabama is still partially segregated; blacks attend church with blacks, and whites attend with whites. Black students attend a local, county public school while white students attend a private school or are shuttled to surrounding schools. Blacks even live primarily in one area of town while whites live in other areas. Why is this critical for this chapter? Well, as a bi-racial child in 1990, I had never experienced anything like this. I attended the all-black high school, and shortly after arriving in Eutaw, my parents began doing ministry work in that town. Here is where the roots start!

I will never forget one hot sunny day as I exited the bus and walked to my grandmother's home on Elm Street where we were living. As I got closer to the house, I saw a tow truck parked next to our 1990 Chevy Trailblazer (loaded, limited edition). Quickly thereafter, the tow truck pulled away and so did the only means of transportation for our family. My father was sitting on the porch of this small 700 sq. ft. foot home, but he was not crying, he wasn't even sad or angry. I remember him looking at me as I walked into the yard and asking how my day was. Well, considering I was the only one in the school who looked like me, had hair like me, had freckles like me, and even talked like me, it was ok. "The kids gave me a nickname today," I said, "oh yeah, what's that?" my father asked. "They now call me white boy!"

In the south, everyone must have a nickname. I actually don't even know the real names of most of the friends I grew up with. Well, my dad laughed and said those kids were clueless and that they'd soon find out that I wasn't just white. As the day went on, he told me the SUV was repossessed and we would get another car soon. In the meantime, we would walk to town and other places that were only 3-4 miles away, if that. My dad looked at me with a look I had never seen before, and he said, "Jeremy, God is going to provide! I don't know how and when, but we will be ok." He later went on to tell me, " I am going to provide your basic needs as a kid, you will be fine, but if you want anything else in life, new shoes, clothes, or other stuff, you will have to work for it and use your own money until things get better for us." I can't tell you that the conversation took root that day; I was still in complete shock and really scared about this entire move and transformation that had recently taken place. However; I can fast-forward about six months and tell you I was then cutting about 12 yards a week with a lawnmower my grandmother bought me as a gift from Langham Motors. I can also tell you I was washing 5–10 cars on Saturday afternoons at my grandmother's house. Finally, I can tell you I was picking up 5–6 pounds of pecans from trees that were on private property (don't tell) and selling them to a local grocery store, Foodland.

As the years went by, I was 14 years old and worked on a farm in Boligee, Alabama for $40 a day (12-hour days). I remember going to a Sandwich Shoppe in our town and asking the owner if he needed help, advertising that I could sweep, clean, or deliver sandwiches. He soon started a delivery service, and a man named Willie who was about 35 years old became my partner as we began delivering sandwiches all over town on my bike or on foot. I then asked the local drug store if I could come by

The Grass is Greener on the Other Side, But it's Synthetic!

at night when they closed and stock the soda machines so the workers didn't have to. I did that for a free 20oz. Coca-Cola (that was like heaven at the time). There are so many other odd jobs I remember, but what really stood out was a man who came in town from Meridian, Mississippi, every week who delivered Coca-Cola products. I asked him if I could work for him and help stock the stores. I was only 15 at the time, and he said, "we don't have room in our truck for you, but if you ride your bike to every stop we make, I can let you unload the truck and stack the sodas with us." Could I? I would love to! I met him every Thursday at 5:30am at the local bait shop (his first stop), and I rode my bike to about 12–15 stores in our town and on the outskirts of our town to unload and stack sodas for $25 a day. It wasn't the money that makes me recall this man—no—it was the spirit he had.

Mr. Jerome was a minister who worked for Coca-Cola during the week to feed his family, but he also held bible study and church and helped others in Meridian,

Mississippi. He talked to me as if I was an adult, he encouraged me and prayed with me and, most of all, he taught me work ethic and customer service. I remember walking into the bait shop one morning with Mr. Jerome, and the owner of the bait shop, an older white man, Mr. Norman Davenport, looked at him and said, "I need all the drinks unloaded and put up by 6am nigger, and you can use your little Half Breed to help you, but he can't walk in my cooler." *Half Breed! Oh now, I'm a dog!* Mr. Jerome looked at Mr. Norman and said, "yes sir, we should be done by then and out your way." *Huh?* Even I knew by then, you can't talk to folks like that, but Mr. Jerome had a bigger plan. He was planting seeds and loving-on Mr. Davenport in hopes that one day his heart would change. He was also planting seeds in me, as I was watching his every move like a hawk.

That summer passed, and I learned more from Mr. Jerome than I ever could have imagined. Other kids in the neighborhood spent their time at the pool, basketball courts, or camps, but not me. I was 15 years old and determined to work 12–15 hours a day to make $50 a day, which was good money in 1993 for a 15-year-old in Eutaw, Alabama. On the surface, you never would have known how hurt I felt at times; you never would have known how tired I really was, or even how scared I was at times. I was trying my best to offset the financial struggle that my parents were having. I wanted to buy my own clothes and shoes to keep up with the other kids so I wouldn't be made fun of or even beat up. I tell people all the time, it was real every day. Not a day went by that I did not try to form a strategy. I didn't know that's what I was doing, but now that I look back, that's all I was doing.

The seeds were being planted: hard work, dedication, customer service, professionalism, love, sacrifice, humility, and many more. What I really want you to take from this story is, I wasn't planting those seeds in myself—no—others were planting them in me, but I had to be present for the seed to be sowed. I had to ask for work at 13, 14, and 15 years old for someone to sow a seed in me. I had to make sacrifices, and sometimes do jobs for FREE just to prove I could do it, such as cutting grass. I recall telling Mr. Marrow on the corner of Highway 43, just beyond my grandmother's home " Sir, I will cut this huge yard for free; if you like it, pay me. If not, I won't ever come back." He became my client for three years when I 13-16 years old. He was also my history teacher and gave me two failing grades, but we never mixed business with school, although maybe I should have tried.

Please catch this concept. For your roots to grow, you must have seeds being sown, which means you must be present or in the presence of seed-sowers. You must also be willing to receive the seed and to keep your soil ready at all times. As a 14, 15, or 16-year-old, I had no idea that I was learning to let the roots form in my life. Those seeds are the result of many successes I have today. Even

The Grass is Greener on the Other Side, But it's Synthetic!

as I write this book almost 25 years later, I thank God for the path he led me on. The journey hasn't always been fun or without difficulties and challenges, but it allowed me to be a greater father, husband, and ultimately citizen in our country. The roots are there, and the results don't always show, but I can rely on those roots any day and know my fruit is plentiful.

In 1993, I went to an office building in our town every Friday to clean, take out trash, and vacuum the floors for Mr. Charles Williams, or "Rev. Charles" as he was affectionately called. I asked him who cleaned his building, to which he replied, "they had a person, but if you really want to make extra money, I will pay you $20 to take out the trash, vacuum the floors, and clean the place up really nice." WOW! $20 for a 2-hour job… oh yeah, I had hit gold there every Friday. Boy, did I get more than my money's worth. Rev. Charles and Mr. Toice Goodson, Sr. talked to me every Friday for about an hour. They shared life stories and lessons that I would later use. I also remember them telling me that if I really wanted to make some money to walk over to Spiller Furniture and ask them if I could wash their windows.

Spiller Furniture was a huge 8,000 sq. ft. store with 7 huge, storefront floor-to-ceiling windows, which were 8 ft. high, but I immediately loved the idea. I formed a plan to speak with the manager and calculated a price of $5 a window for a total profit of $35. As I continued to think of my plan, I realized I could serve two clients, Rev. Charles for $20 a week and Spiller Furniture for $35. As I entered the furniture store, I immediately met with Mrs. Donna Sellers, she was and still is an awesome woman with an incredible heart. I went over my plan with her, and she admitted, "Well Jeremy, I don't have money to do that, but if you really want to do it, I can pay you out of my pocket." *Well, of course, I want to do it.* I cleaned the windows, which took about two and a half hours to finish. Mrs. Donna handed me a ten-dollar bill, and I almost cried. I thanked her and told her I'd be back. I got on my bike and rode the two miles home to Elm Street and remember thinking, *that lady gave me ten bucks for all that.*

As time went on, I continued to clean both Rev. Charles' office and the windows at Spiller Furniture, as I was in no position to turn down $10. Mrs. Donna later asked if I knew how to cut grass and solicited me to cut her family's yard to make some extra money. *Cut grass? Do I know how to cut grass?* That was my specialty at the time and where my roots started so, of course, I took the job. I cut her yard that weekend for $25, and Mrs. Donna and her husband, Mike, loved it so much that they asked me to put them on my list of clients. Here is where it gets good. Mrs. Donna lived about five miles from my house, I never traveled that far to cut grass because I didn't want to push the mower, weed eater, rake, gas can, and shovel that far. As I started cutting her yard, her neighbors stopped by and asked if I could come to their home next. After about two weeks, I had six yards in Mrs. Donna's neighborhood, and each was paying me $25–40 dollars per cut.

Remember, this all started with a $10 dollar window cleaning, right? Wrong! This all began with Rev. Charles and Mr. Goodson encouraging me to approach Spiller Furniture about cleaning their windows. These men planted a seed in me, and I had to do the work and set the roots. Sure, I was not initially happy with making $10 for roughly two hours of work cleaning windows, but that lead to me making $200 each Saturday cutting yards in Mrs. Donna's neighborhood.

In 2017, my path again crossed with Mrs. Donna, who still worked for the same furniture store. The owner of Spiller Furniture Mr. Shane Spiller, hired me to conduct a leadership conference for all his staff in Tuscaloosa, Alabama. As Mrs. Donna entered the room, I knew it was going to be a great reunion, as it'd been 23 years since we'd seen each other. I was right! She lost it; she teared up and, of course, so did I. Mrs. Donna planted a seed in my life that allowed me to come back and teach her company on leadership! WOW! If that doesn't give you chills, you might be dead. I blessed Mrs. Donna that day with a gift card to dinner, and I told her in front of her peers how much she meant to my life. Her gesture of love for a young man who was really trying to survive had an impact she never knew about. The seed took root, and the results didn't show immediately, but they were there. Mrs. Donna had no idea how much I appreciate her, and I was so glad I had the chance to say thank you. I want to go a step further and thank her in this book as well. Mrs. Donna Sellers of Eutaw, Alabama, I love you and value everything you have done for my family and all the families of Greene County, Alabama.

So, consider this: stop trying to show others what your fruit is, and let them see it for themselves. Ensure your roots are solid so when the storms of life come, you are grounded and unmovable. Never underestimate where God is leading you, or who he is using to plant those seeds into your life. Mrs. Donna was so thrilled and happy for my success in life, it was almost as if I were her son.

Roots take time to grow deep; there are no quick ways or shortcuts to success in life. Success—long lasting success—comes with strong roots and continual re-seeding. As you consider that, you must also know your environment and what your purpose is in that area. What are you there to give and/or get, and how can you maximize the environment and situation you're in?

Chapter Three

STOP CUTTING SO SHORT, AND KNOW YOUR ENVIRONMENT

One of the worst things you can do to a yard is cut it too short in hotter months. This was an early mistake I made with my yard when I first started. Sure, the grass looks good when you cut it, but cutting it too short causes the healthy parts of the grass to be exposed to direct sunlight, causing the soil to dry faster and become damaged. The biggest challenge I had when I first started cutting my yard was, I didn't know the environment. I had no idea what kinds of grass were planted, how much Ph was in the soil, or even what the soil content was.

Although this sounds very deep, or in the vein of science, it's extremely important to know the soil/environment in which your grass grows.

It's also extremely important to let grass grow and take root *before* you cut it. Many people see two-to-three inches of nice, pretty green grass, and they quickly begin cutting it (that was me), trying to make the yard look good with lines and designs. However, the real goal is to allow it to grow about 4–6 inches and then only cut 1–2 inches off. The process of pruning the grass and trimming just the top causes it to grow faster, but also gives the roots time to grow deeper and stronger.

This is true in life; you must know the environment you are in, and you have to let your roots grow deep before you start trimming or picking the fruit of your labor. So many times, I see people who want results so badly that they begin to alter the process, rather than letting things play-out on their own. In the process of growing grass, you must let the roots grow deep and really form before you can start cutting the grass. There will be plenty of time to cut, but you will never get the results you want if the roots are not strong and secure.

When I ruined my yard at my first house, I finally called for help. John, from AMG, came to fix it and said he knew the area very well and had worked with homes around me, but he still wanted to take a soil sample and come back with a treatment plan. I was so impressed that John would even consider doing that, as many people usually assume they know it all, become reactionary, and fail to properly study and research first. I am sure John could have put some chemicals down and given me some immediate results within days, but he knew I wanted lasting results. He knew I wanted results that were going to have an impact for as long as I owned the home. When John came back, he had a plan to attack my environment, and it worked within 30 days. He told me when to cut, water, and seed the yard. Although others were not doing what I was doing, even in the same environment, I had to follow the instructions of the SME.

As you think about your life, I want you to consider something. How did you know how to be a great parent, or a great employee/worker? Who showed you, or taught you, how to be a good citizen? If you grew up in the South but later moved to the North like I did, how did you know how to adjust to the weather, snow, and different driving conditions? In life, some things are instincts, some things are responsive impulses, and some things we really need demonstrated and taught. If you seek to be great at anything, you must have all three. You need great instincts to be a business owner, leader, parent, husband/wife, or anything else you desire. You also need responsive impulses and rapid decision making at times to be great. Most of all, you need examples.

Ninety percent of us learn through demonstration and examples. As a kid, you didn't become potty-trained by just having your mom or dad say, "go pee." They actually demonstrated it, and they even gave you rewards when you got it right. On this journey, I have found when you know your environment well and plant your seeds in that environment with wisdom, you grow. Each environment is different, just as each seed is different.

As a young man, I became a leader in the Navy very quickly. I was promoted each of my first four years, and I was also responsible for leading teams when we deployed. I remember coming home and attempting to apply my leadership traits and tools on my wife. Wow, what a major mistake! I seriously loved all the things I was learning and how we acquired results, even in difficult situations. I loved, and still love, leadership training and teaching just as much as I love being a leader. I remember telling my wife, we would be a great couple if she just understood the seven habits of a highly effective leader. She turned to me and said, "I know the five seasonings to put in this fried chicken to make you happy. Leave me alone with that leadership stuff." I had to adjust my seeds to the home environment, which was totally different than my military environment or even my business environment. Just as John came to my home and took a soil sample of my yard, I had to take an assessment of each environment I operated in and make the according adjustments for that area. The worst thing you can do in life is not change! Here are some questions for you to consider:

1. Do I try to make things fit my environment, or do I conform to the environment in place?
2. Now that I know my seeds/gifts/talents/expertise, does the environment I'm in accept that, or should I seek a new environment?
3. What can I do to help facilitate change in my environments, or is it even possible?

One of the biggest challenges most business owners or C-Level leaders have is family. Yes, I know if you run a successful company and secure financial stability, idealistically you should not have family issues. Wrong! You see most leaders struggle with family because 90 percent of their day is filled with decisions, timelines, deadlines, and expectations. In our families, most of the same is day-to-day and very unpredictable. Who knows what your 11-year-old is going to do today at camp? *What's for dinner, I cooked last night, take out the trash, you missed my mom's birthday again, and you do know we are supposed to meet the Hawkins Family for dinner at 6:30 tonight, right?* Leaders who lead all day typically don't want to come home and lead much of anything. However, the family environment lends itself for leaders to lead, and most spouses and children love when leaders lead effectively. What they don't love is when you try to lead your family like you lead your staff.

Let me encourage all leaders in this; know the environment and know how to apply different and often unique leadership traits. Don't deploy sternness when meekness could have been expressed. Don't talk when others really want you to simply listen, smile, and nod. When John came to fix the problem in my yard, the first thing he said was, "tell me what's going on, and what have you done so far." He was the expert; he knew exactly what was going on and he could see clearly what I had done. But, he was forming a collaborative relationship with me and allowing me to be a part of the solution, because clearly, I was the problem. I know many of you may be thinking, *wow, Jeremy, you're asking a lot of me to change my ways in each environment.* No, not really. It's not that you must change your ways, as much as you must understand what that environment is doing and how best to get the results you want. Sometimes you must adapt, sometimes others must adapt. The key is knowing that! Once you know and accept your environment, your life will be so much better.

Chapter Four

REST, HEAL, AND RE-SEED

Grass really needs time to rest! There is no way that you can keep adding chemicals, cutting it, watering it, and expect to get results. At some point, the grass simply needs time to grow. Not only did John share this with me, my friends and neighbors began to tell me the same thing. Based on what I had done to the yard, it needed time to rest and heal. Once that process was complete, I really needed to re-seed. Although my yard was not a major disaster, it was bad enough that it needed to heal.

Sometimes in life, we must take time to rest, heal, and re-group. I find that so many people, including myself, feel that we must be doing something all the time. We feel that if we are not working or doing something productive, then we must not be effective. Some of my greatest work and most powerful moments in life are when I find time to rest and walk away from life for a day or so. I plan healing/rejuvenation periods to ensure I can balance my life and the many challenges and opportunities that may present themselves. I also need time to regroup from the day-to-day grind of life. Just as I gave my yard a rest and stopped cutting the grass for a while, in that same manner you need to rest. For my business folks out there, don't be afraid to walk away for a moment and give the deal time to work. Don't be so afraid that if you're not there, it won't work. I have found that distance often brings closure and unity. Oftentimes, when you have distance, you have time to evaluate the situation and the circumstances surrounding it. You have time to think through your approach and what worked and didn't work.

I had a chance to feed my yard chemicals but also time to research what each chemical really meant and did for my type of yard. I also had time to see how the yard would react without chemicals. Most leaders never give their staff or team time to think independently, they feel they always must provide a solution or a certain type of approach. Great leaders, great spouses, and successful people realize they are only a component of the solutions they face, and many people, other than them, play a part in the complete approach. This is very evident in sports, Corporate America, and great educational institutions. During the healing process of everything you face in life, you really need to consider several things:

1. What caused this to take place?
2. Once my healing is complete, am I prepared to move on?
3. What changes need to be made to ensure success?

Once you answer these three basic questions, you certainly have a stronger foundation for progress. There will always be moments in life when you must adjust and readjust your plan, but the foundation for success and the recipe should not change.

Once I gave my yard a rest and allowed it to heal, I then took the time to aerate the lawn and re-seed. Aeration involves perforating the soil with small holes to allow air, water, and nutrients to penetrate the roots. This process helps the lawn get stronger and healthier. Shortly after aeration, I would normally re-seed and ensure I have the maximum amount of grass roots growing in my yard. This is also the time that I normally dig-up old grass and pick weeds and wildflowers.

Whenever you want something to be great, you absolutely need to poke holes in it to allow the proper flow of nutrients. Whenever I come up with a business plan/concept, I typically hand it to five-to-seven leaders/experienced CEOs and have them poke holes in my processes, plan, approach, and overall product. I then give it to 10-15 potential clients/customers and have them poke holes in the new plan. Finally, once I have finished that process, I present the final concept to all parties and add in 10-15 additional folks who have never seen or heard about it. Many business owner or leaders call this process a pilot phase or approach. I believe that in life, we all need to re-seed at times. We need to pick the old grass out, kill the weeds, and plant new seeds. As I am writing this book, I am on my eighth company. Each company that I have started, worked with, and/or sold has gotten better and better through the entire process.

Every day, I seek to learn something new, find a better way, or tweak my approach to help others. I don't always re-seed immediately because I want to ensure that something is truly dead before I discard it. Many people are so interested in re-seeding that they forget they already spent a ton of time, money, and energy planting the seeds that are already in the ground. Let me encourage you in this; don't be so quick to give up on something that seems dead when it just needs to be aerated. Marriages don't just fail, businesses don't just file bankruptcy, and leaders don't just give up. Ensure that when you decide to re-seed that you have understood all the time it will take to grow the new. Re-seeding for me is also done in conjunction with areas of focus. I don't normally re-seed my entire yard, I take a section or two and give those areas care, attention, and love to ensure I observe things going wrong as they occur. It's difficult to control an entire lawn that's out of control rather than one or two spots. Once those spots are healthy and I understand what it takes for them to be healthy, I then move on to fix the rest of the yard. Answer these questions:

1. Do I need to re-seed my situation, or do I need to give it more attention?
2. Have I taken time to heal from the previous situation before I walk into the new one?
3. When do I take time to rest and reflect on my situations and life?

Chapter Five

SYNTHETIC IS NOT REAL - YOU KNOW THAT, RIGHT?

This chapter is why I wanted to write this book. Not only does it reflect the title, it reflects real life in every situation. I would encourage you to read this chapter at least two times.

As the years went by, and my yard was well established, my wife and I decided to prepare to sell our home. We had lived there for 13 years, and it was time to move and explore another area. As we did our research, I never looked at curb appeal because I knew I could change it, or improve it just as I'd done with this home. Our real estate agent, Mr. Mike Spurgeon of Remax, told us he had an awesome house for us to see, and everything was move-in ready.

Upon seeing the house, he was correct; everything was move-in ready except the yard. For an amateur/average person, the yard was good; it was green, and the grass was cut, but per my standard's the yard was falling apart. It was on the verge of breaking down, and the previous owners had only done enough to ensure the house sold. I could see the grubs, weeds, dryness and, most of all, the many variations of grass (tall fescue, fine fescue, bluegrass, and a little zoysia grass). I knew the previous owners didn't have a clue, but why would they. Most people have no idea what type of grass they have, they just want it green.

Ensuring a green and nicely cut yard is what 95 percent of us want. As I began to research the best approach for my yard, I decided to attend a home and garden expo at the local fairgrounds. I knew if I could get some information, take some soil samples, and get quotes from landscapers, I could have my yard fixed in less than a year. It was at that expo that I had a bright idea. I planned to live in this house for at least 10-15 years, so why not invest in turf? Everyone was using turf for sports fields at schools, recreation centers, and even NFL teams. Surely someone at the home expo would tell me about a turf field option. Well, they certainly did. I recall seeing several booths for commercial turf field products, and one company had a home photo of a client who installed it at his home. Boy, was I excited, I had hit a homerun!

The neighbors were going to be in awe of my yard, and I would never have to cut grass or hire a landscaper again. As I approached the booth, I smelled the aroma of rubber bands, or what seemed like new tires. I introduced myself to Seth, the sales representative, and told him I wanted to buy a turf product for my home. We discussed products and a price, he found my house on Google Maps, and he asked "when would you like to start?" just like a typical salesman. I looked him in the eye and said "tomorrow, where do I sign?" I think he was surprised and happy at the same time. Just 17 minutes ago, he was eating a fairground corndog, and now he was making a sale for over $20,000 (luckily, I got a military discount). We signed the paperwork, and he told me someone would be in touch soon. I was so happy as I finished walking around that expo that I bought some other items and got a hot dog and Bud Light (relax church folks, it's only one beer, lol).

During my drive home, I decided I wasn't going to tell anyone, not even my wife. I wanted everything to be a surprise. No one needed to know we were getting a turf field as our home yard, or did they? Well, yes, they did. There was no way the Homeowners Association was going to let me install this without approval—who did I think I was, a homeowner? Sad, but true. Living in a community such as ours has its pros and cons, but this one was going to be easy. At the same time I was doing all this, I also decided to get back into coaching high school football, as if I needed more on my plate.

I loved the excitement of high school football, and a good friend of mine, Coach Kenny Lucas, was coaching at Annapolis Area Christian School, a private school in Maryland. I decided to jump in and get my hands dirty with him. As we began to talk about football and the Xs and Os, we also talked about a new field that we wanted built for the kids. The program was experiencing success, but we did not have a home field to play on. There was an indoor turf field for practice, but it was not big enough for football. There was an outdoor grass field, but it was not set to play high school games. I walked in one day and told the guys that I had the perfect solution.

I was getting turf installed at my home, so why don't we call the same company and see if they can work out a deal for us here at the school. Great idea, right? No! Coach Lucas laughed and said, "you are getting what?" I went on to explain to him why I was getting turf installed at my home. Coach laughed again and said, "I heard you man, but I think you're crazy!" He definitely thought

I was; no one had seen this before, and I was going to change the way yards were designed and the way people looked at yard care. I was also going to have the nicest looking yard, greenest grass, and the best edges anyone could want. "Jeremy, you mean to tell me you're going to dig up your grass, put down fake grass, and let your kids play on that"? I was totally confused by the question. "What do you mean?" I asked.

Coach Lucas went on to tell me there are certainly good things about turf fields, but you don't want that in your home yard. You want real grass, something your kids can run and play on and not burn their feet; something you can fall on and not get hurt or rubber burn; you also don't want to walk on synthetic grass when it's wet because it's extremely slippery. He went on to tell me how real grass has a bounce to it, the earth has soil that is soft and forgiving. If you fall or jump on synthetic grass, you may injure yourself every time. Sure football, soccer, lacrosse, and field hockey players play on it, but they have spikes in their cleats, they have knee pads, elbow pads, and other protective gear. You don't want your kids and family playing or relaxing on that stuff. Wow! He just killed all my joy but, more importantly, I needed to see if I could get my $5,000 deposit back.

I immediately called Seth and told him I was not going to order the turf. I am so glad I didn't have to do that in person. Seth didn't respond, "hello, are you there?" Seth came back on the line and said, "I am here, I understand and it's sad that we have to cancel." He was very professional and told me there would be a processing fee of $199 but, if I wanted, I could talk to a manager and try to get that back. I told Seth, it was totally my mistake and that $199 was acceptable, and I'd have to eat my loss.

Now what do I do? I just spent the last 30 days giving up on my yard because I was getting turf. The turf had all the features I wanted, and it looked good, felt good (at the expo, in a climate- controlled farmhouse), it even smelled fine, except for the slight rubber scent. I was semi- devastated; I needed to come up with a plan and fix this yard or else we were going to be in trouble next year.

Doesn't this story sound familiar to our lives? Don't we look at things that are nicer, bigger, better, faster and, of course, more than what we have? The grass was greener, but it was synthetic, and synthetic grass has so many challenges and poses issues that I never anticipated. Who would have known that every two years I would have to pay $2,300 to get new rubber pellets spread throughout the yard because the other ones would have washed away? I never would have thought about the softness of the natural soil verse the hardness of this turf. If it had not been for Coach Lucas and his comments, I would have never considered the pads that athletes wear while performing on turf fields versus my children wanting to run and play in the yard barefoot.

In life, sometimes we want what others have; we see the results or the newness, but we don't seem to comprehend all that pieces of the puzzle. In marriages, I have seen people divorce each other because they wanted someone more attractive, more educated, wealthier, or even more dynamic in the bedroom (it's true). But what they miss is the true meaning of love and commitment; they miss the total person or the total package.

Ninety percent of us think in a selfish manner when we see others with success or accomplishments. Very few people can feel excited for you and bless you at the same time. When we think of the story of the turf field, imagine if I had gone through with my decision. Imagine if I installed the turf and all the challenges began to present themselves, how much more would that effect other things in my life? Something as simple as grass versus turf could have easily torn my marriage apart, hurt my children and pets, but also caused me to be very prideful and arrogant. I can imagine how I would feel if my kids told me, "Daddy, we don't like this fake grass, it burns our feet, and we can't play in the yard with our friends barefoot." I could only imagine if my wife or friends started mocking me because of my selfish decision to have the best.

In my eyes, I could justify why I needed and wanted this, and how this was better in the long run. How devastated I would have been if I'd dug up $20,000 of turf just to install $2,000 of sod, or $800 of grass seeds. In that same likeness, I want you to consider something for a minute. How many times have you tried something, purchased something, or even gone somewhere because you saw it done by others and you thought, *I deserve that!* How many times have you seen someone get a new car, house, spouse, job, or even a bonus and you ask yourself, *why can't I get that?* How many times have you been close to someone and suddenly, they experience success or happiness, but it doesn't include you, and you thought it should? Finally, how many times have you seen someone that you knew didn't deserve what they had or what was given to them? Sure, we all have those moments. We all live in a very judgmental world and, sadly, we use our perception more than we use our heart. We also chase fame and fortune more than we chase peace, love and joy. We have become a society that has turned from God and turned to stuff.

Material things, titles, fortune, and other irrelevant stuff has replaced our desire to want relationships, joy, and peace in the world. When I think about the synthetic grass, I think, *wow, why didn't I see that?* Clearly, I was blinded by my desire to want something for a different purpose than what it was intended for. Sure, Seth, the turf salesman, was only doing his job; if I wanted to put it on the moon, he would have sold it to me. Nevertheless, I needed a friend, a coach, a person to say, "Jeremy are you crazy"?

It wasn't until I listened to that voice of reasoning and that expert at the time, that I realized I was making a huge mistake. Sure, the grass was greener, but it was also fake. Fake things simulate the real, which means they will never serve the same purpose or give you the same benefits as the real. In life, you have to realize that fake things only last for a period of time. No matter how much time you put into a fake relationship, it will never be real. No matter how much attention you give a fake situation, it will never get better.

When synthetic grass was first created in the 1960s, it was not intended to replace real grass; it was intended to serve as a maintenance-free product that could withstand sports in an arena. Even today in 2019, we have more residential products that can be used; you will never replace the realness of grass. Even the best product on the market now does not have the capability to stand up to real grass.

As you experience life more and more, you will encounter people who are only interested in synthetic grass; they want it quick, fast, and in a hurry. These kinds of people want what they see and don't care about the process, down falls, or even the pain associated with results. Their only mission in life is to create the appearance of having greener grass than you and others. I watch these people stand in lines for the new cell phones, the latest shoes, or even the next great movie, so they can say they had it/saw it first. They are more consumed with one-upping someone or something that they never really find their true purpose in life or even their real passion.

I would be wrong if I did not give a suggestion on how to fix this, if only just a little. Consider this; nothing that God has for you can be consumed by someone or something else! What is designated for you will be for you as you prepare for it and proclaim it. Stop taking time out of your life to be consumed with what others have, did, or said.

There is a prayer my dad made me repeat every day before I went to school, and I still say it today: *God, grant me the serenity to accept the things I cannot change, courage to change the things I can, and wisdom to know the difference.* Most of us lack wisdom when it comes to knowing what we can and cannot change. If you capture this as your focus each day, you will be great! You will also have love, joy, and peace in your life. I am not saying you won't have struggles and trials, but I can promise you will pull through them all in peace, especially once you realize your true purpose and calling in life.

Leave the synthetic grass alone and focus on growing your own grass. Ensure your roots are strong and you continue to water and feed the grass you seek to grow. Never let someone walk on your grass and cause you to quit or be so discouraged that you give up. Please remember that droughts come, and sometimes you must endure for a season until the water starts to flow again. Don't become complacent in your good times and forget the drought may and will come. Plan accordingly, and be sure to sow seeds in the lives of others so their yards can blossom like your yard. Leave your selfish ways behind, and seek a new beginning in life, it's never too late to re-seed or sod your yard. Finally, don't hoard the knowledge of how to care for the grass; seek others to share this with, and ensure they understand everyone grows differently, but basic principles are still required to achieve success. When sowing into others and giving unto others, your life will be blessed beyond measure.

Here are some next steps:

1. Get planted, and ensure your roots are healthy in all your dealings.
2. Seek to love more so we can make this a better world to live in.
3. Once you have gained enough knowledge and experience, please share it willingly.
4. Don't always look to get something, seek to give and you will get.
5. Read John 3:16 from the Bible, and find a relationship with Christ.

God has blessed me tremendously in life. I can't imagine what life would be like if I never went through the storms and trails. Let me encourage you in this, don't ever underestimate the unique position or circumstances that you are afforded. Nothing that was ever great was made without pain, sacrifice and even some set-backs. When you see greener grass in others, celebrate them and never assume you know their roots. When you see synthetic grass understand….. It won't last, it's FAKE!

Thank you for reading my book, Jeremy Allen Sr.

Email me at Jeremy@jmichaelsolutions.com and let me know how this book has impacted your life.

For speaking and booking events, please email me and let's help change lives.

Made in the USA
Lexington, KY
20 November 2019